THE LIST

Compiled by the Editors of VH1

POCKET BOOKS   Music First®

NEW YORK   LONDON   TORONTO   SYDNEY   SINGAPORE

Acknowledgments

Many thanks to Lauren Zalaznick and Michael A. Rosen for taking the time to see this book through.

Special thanks to: Nancy Abbott-Young, Ken Baron, Ivy Baron, Jacqueline Bender, Richard Buhrman, Mary Bourke, Liz Brooks, Christine Carlson, Tommy Cody, Myra Correa, Wallie Einenkel, Bill Flanagan, Mike Garvey, Jeff Gaspin, Bruce Gillmer, Fred Graver, Michael Grimes, Monica Halpert, Penny Haynes, Anastasia Hays, Leah Horwitz, Jacob Hoye, Jade Hoye, Ryan Ingrasin, Mimi James, Kari Johnson, Bernie Kaminsky, Catherine Kerr, Andy Lassner, Jane Lipsitz, Dean Lubensky, Chris McGhee, Lisa Masuda, Patrick Murphy, Kay O'Connell, Donna O'Neill, Cassandra Patterson, Jaime Putorti, Mary Russell, Ann Sarnoff, Barry Scott, Lisa Silfen, Jennifer Stilson, Michelle Stuart, John Sykes, Donald Sylvie, Kara Welsh, Eric Wybenga, Rachel Zalis, and all the fans who went online at VH1.com and voted for their favorites in all of the categories.

Special thanks to the crew and especially the fantastic and energetic hosts and guests of the show.

All of the polling information in *The List* book was compiled by VH1.com and its users. You can play along with *The List* everyday on VH1.com.

Photography credits:
Frank Micelotta: 14, 16, 63, 137, and 151
Paul McCallum: Title Page, 27, 28, 45, 61, 67, 71, 72, 74, 78, 89, 105, 124, 129, and 152
Sticky Fingers album cover courtesy of Virgin Benelux B.V.
House of the Holy album cover courtesy of Atlantic Records

An *Original* Publication of VH1 BOOKS/POCKET BOOKS

POCKET BOOKS, a division of Simon & Schuster, Inc.
1230 Avenue of the Americas, New York, NY 10020

ISBN: 0-7434-1799-2

First VH1 Books/Pocket Books trade paperback printing January 2001

10 9 8 7 6 5 4 3 2 1

POCKET and colophon are registered trademarks of Simon & Schuster, Inc.

Cover and book design by Charles Kreloff

Printed in the U.S.A.

inTrodUction

The first thing that hits a first-time visitor to VH1's Times Square headquarters is all the music. It grabs you when you step off the elevator and follows you down the hall. There's music in the waiting areas, music in the cubicles, even music in the bathrooms. The people who work at VH1 may look like grownups (well, most of them) but they keep the volume up like tenth graders.

Walk through their offices and you're struck by the piles of CDs, the photos of rock stars, the autographed set-lists and drumheads and guitars. VH1 is a place where adults can get away with putting posters on their walls and cranking their stereos up to eleven. And get paid for it.

The neighbors don't even yell, "Turn it down!" They either yell "Turn it up" or drown you out with their own selections.

When such people talk—or shout as the case may be—it is usually about music. And a lot of the regular cafeteria conversation is about music. Like obsessive fans everywhere, the VH1 crew love to make lists. They argue about who was better—Prince or Hendrix? Dylan or R.E.M.? Joni Mitchell or Alanis Morissette? These arguments do not seem to break down along any conventional lines of gender, race, or age. You're as likely to see a 40-year-old white male orating on the virtues of

Li'l Kim as you are to find a young woman in hip-hop headgear making the case for the Beatles.

At some point one of these bright executives—perhaps in order to justify drawing a salary from all these lunchroom debates—came up with the idea of polishing up the process and putting it on the air. Wouldn't it be fun, it was proposed, to do a regular series in which all sorts of famous people argued about music—a steel cage death match to determine who was really sexier—Jennifer Lopez or Madonna; which was a better single "Won't Get Fooled Again" or "Smells like Teen Spirit"? Who's a greater diva—Streisand or Aretha?

So was born *The List*—and the arguments in the VH1 hallways spilled out into America. Pretty soon the channel was being buried in letters and e-mails railing in fury against the choices made on the air ("How can you say Celine Dion is a better singer than Garth Brooks?" "What kind of moron thinks *Led Zeppelin IV* beats *Thriller*?") The VH1 crowd had succeeded in dragging millions of viewers into their never-ending argument.

This book is intended to give all those civilians a voice. The people have spoken. These lists were compiled from the opinions of VH1 viewers from all over the country who cast their votes for their favorites at VH1.com, and those viewers deserve our sincerest thanks for making this book possible.

Reading through this book, you may (and you will!) disagree with many of the choices and the order in which they appear. That's why for each category you'll find a space to create your own list. We encourage you to do so. Throughout the book you will also find quotes, facts, and quantitative lists that we think will make this book fun to read and reference.

Finally, we hope that you find this book as enjoyable to read as we did while making our show and compiling this book.

—VH1

THE LIST

○─[beSt '80s

1 "Every Breath You Take" The Police

2 "Sweet Child o' Mine" Guns N' Roses

3 "Another Brick in the Wall" Pink Floyd

4 "I Still Haven't Found What I'm Looking For" U2

5 "Livin' on a Prayer" Bon Jovi

6 "Hungry Like the Wolf" Duran Duran

7 "Born in the USA" Bruce Springsteen

8 "Sweet Dreams (Are Made of This)" Eurythmics

9 "Like a Virgin" Madonna

10 "Jump" Van Halen

Just Missed
"Sexual Healing" Marvin Gaye

❝ I was in an unemployment office when I first began acting and we were waiting for three, four hours. There was a middle-aged black guy in the back and he just started screaming 'I want my money! I want my money now!' He said, 'I was a vet. I fought for our country. I want my money!' So we're like, 'whatever, this guy's bugging out,' and all of a sudden, he started singing 'Born in the USA' loud. It sent chills down your spine. The crowd parted, this guy walked up to the front of the line. They gave him his money and he walked out. I had tears in my eyes and the crowd applauded. ❞

—DAVID ALAN GRIER

FaCT
"Every Breath You Take" was the number one single of 1983 and the only Police song to reach number one on *Billboard*'s Top 40 chart. It was also the foundation for Puff Daddy's and Faith Evan's number one single "I'll Be Missing You" which spent eleven weeks at number one in 1997.

soNg

" If you can't get lucky to this song, you can't get lucky. "
—Frank DeCaro, *The Daily Show* movie critic, on "Sexual Healing"

thE biGGest HitS of the '80s		(weeks at number one)
1. "Physical"	Olivia Newton-John	10
2. "Bette Davis Eyes"	Kim Carnes	9
"Endless Love"	Diana Ross and Lionel Richie	9
3. "Every Breath You Take"	The Police	8
4. "Ebony and Ivory"	Stevie Wonder and Paul McCartney	7
5. "Billie Jean"	Michael Jackson	7

Source: *Billboard*

mEn aT WorK leaD siNger coLiN haY's liSt

1. "Every Breath You Take"   The Police
2. "Sexual Healing"   Marvin Gaye
3. "Always on My Mind"   Willie Nelson

doN dOKken's lisT

1. "Hot for Teacher"   Van Halen
2. "I Still Haven't Found What I'm Looking For"   U2
3. "Welcome to the Jungle"   Guns N' Roses

My List

1
2
3
4
5
6
7
8
9
10

Best '80s SoNg

⊶[bEst '7os

1. **Led Zeppelin**
2. **The Eagles**
3. **Queen**
4. **Fleetwood Mac**
5. **Pink Floyd**
6. **Bee Gees**
7. **Elton John**
8. **Billy Joel**
9. **KISS**
10. **David Bowie**

Just Missed
Bruce Springsteen

FaCT

Led Zeppelin reigned supreme in the seventies with six number one albums. Their 1973 tour of the States broke many box-office records throughout the country and by the mid-seventies they were considered the most popular band in the world.

❝KISS understood that visual things you take home are the gifts they can never take away from you.❞

—Garth Brooks, VH1 interview

bANd or artiSt

rIck spRinGField'S lisT

1. Led Zeppelin
2. David Bowie
3. Stevie Wonder

joHn taYloR's lISt

1. David Bowie
2. Queen
3. Chic

❝I like Elton John. Elton John had homies in the hood singing 'Bennie and the Jets.' You can't front on Elton John.❞

—Ice-T

❝[David Bowie] carried the '70s.❞

—Duran Duran's John Taylor

My List

1 _____
2 _____
3 _____
4 _____
5 _____
6 _____
7 _____
8 _____
9 _____
10 _____

best '70s Band or artiSt

baNd or aRtiST inflUeNtial

1. **Madonna**

2. **The Beatles**

3. **Kurt Cobain**

4. **Elvis Presley**

5. **David Bowie**

6. **Elton John**

7. **Boy George**

8. **Michael Jackson**

9. **Cher**

10. **Cyndi Lauper**

Just Missed
Alice Cooper; Marilyn Manson

fAct

Madonna inspired the famous Madonna-wannabes with her distinct early look. Later, she modeled for Versace, strutted the runway for Jean-Paul Gaultier and appeared on the cover of *Vogue*.

" David [Bowie] knows what it takes to be a rock star. He first started out in his dress and he took it off. And when he put on those pants, he started marching, darling! He knows what it takes. He's a showman. "

—Little Richard

whO mADe thE MOst fasHion stAtemEnt

vaNilLA icE's LIst

1. Elvis Presley
2. Jimi Hendrix
3. Madonna

meliSSa riVers's wOrst drEssed artIst liSt

1. Boy George
2. Dolly Parton
3. Tommy Lee

facT

A white rhinestone glove owned by Michael Jackson sold for $28,050 in December of 1991. In 1997, an afghan coat worn by John Lennon on the cover of the Beatles's *Magical Mystery Tour* album (1967) was bought for $57,750 on behalf of his son, Julian.

Source: *Guinness World Records 2000*

"[Kurt Cobain] basically exterminated the hair bands, which was a good thing."

—Jason Falkner, musician

My List

1.
2.
3.
4.
5.
6.
7.
8.
9.
10.

⊶[bEst '6os

1 *Revolver* — The Beatles

2 *The Doors* — The Doors

3 *Led Zeppelin II* — Led Zeppelin

4 *Are You Experienced?* — Jimi Hendrix Experience

5 *Pet Sounds* — The Beach Boys

6 *Tommy* — The Who

7 *Creedence Clearwater Revival* — Creedence Clearwater Revival

8 *Sounds of Silence* — Simon and Garfunkel

9 *Let It Bleed* — The Rolling Stones

10 *Crosby, Stills and Nash* — Crosby, Stills and Nash

Just Missed
Blonde on Blonde — Bob Dylan

❝As soon as the first chord [hits] it just grabs you, it goes straight for the jugular, and it just kind of holds you there until the record's finished.❞

—Green Day's Billy Joe, on *Revolver*, VH1 interview

David Alan Grier and David Duchovny

14

alBum

beStselliNg albUms fRom thE '6os

1.	*The Beatles (The White Album)*	The Beatles
2.	*Led Zeppelin II*	Led Zeppelin
3.	*Abbey Road*	The Beatles
3.	*Sgt. Pepper's Lonely Hearts Club Band*	The Beatles

Source: RIAA

daVid DUchovNy's liSt of albuMs eveRyonE shOuld oWn

1. *Songs in the Key of Life* — Stevie Wonder
2. *The Beatles (The White Album)* — The Beatles
3. *Sticky Fingers* — The Rolling Stones

"People are still trying to make that record today, thirty years later."

—Elvis Costello, on *Revolver*, VH1 interview

faCT

The American version of *Revolver* had three fewer songs than the British version. "I'm Only Sleeping," "And Your Bird Can Sing," and "Doctor Robert" were all removed from the American version as they appeared on *"Yesterday. . . and Today,"* an album released only in the U.S.

My List

1.
2.
3.
4.
5.
6.
7.
8.
9.
10.

15

Best '6os alBum

O—[beSt '6os

1 "(I Can't Get No) Satisfaction" — The Rolling Stones

2 "Hey Jude" — The Beatles

3 "Light My Fire" — The Doors

4 "Respect" — Aretha Franklin

5 "California Dreamin'" — The Mamas and the Papas

6 "Like a Rolling Stone" — Bob Dylan

7 "(Sittin' On) The Dock of the Bay" — Otis Redding

8 "Good Vibrations" — The Beach Boys

9 "My Generation" — The Who

10 "Born to Be Wild" — Steppenwolf

Just Missed
"Me and Bobby McGee" — Janis Joplin

"When I was a kid I memorized the 'na na na na' part, I was a bright child, but my mom's name was Judy and so she said it was her when I was very young."

—David Spade, on "Hey Jude"

Just Shoot Me's David Spade

soNg

thE bigGeSt hiTs oF tHe '6os (weeks at number one)

1. The theme from "A Summer Place"	Percy Faith and His Orchestra	9
2. "Tossin' and Turnin'"	Bobby Lewis	7
"I Want to Hold Your Hand"	The Beatles	7
"I'm a Believer"	The Monkees	7
3. "Aquarius/Let the Sunshine In"	The Fifth Dimension	6

Source: *Billboard*

❝You were going to do things that people said you couldn't do. You were going to meet the girl. You were going to win the golden ring. You were going to take the prize. 'My Generation' became that kind of call for that generation.❞

—Jon Bon Jovi, VH1 interview

My List

1.
2.
3.
4.
5.
6.
7.
8.
9.
10.

best '6os song

bEst '70s

1 *Hotel California*   The Eagles

2 *Dark Side of the Moon*   Pink Floyd

3 *Led Zeppelin IV*   Led Zeppelin

4 *Rumours*   Fleetwood Mac

5 *Saturday Night Fever*   Bee Gees

6 *Born to Run*   Bruce Springsteen

7 *Bridge Over Troubled Water*   Simon and Garfunkel

8 *Who's Next*   The Who

9 *Off the Wall*   Michael Jackson

10 *Tapestry*   Carole King

Just Missed
Songs in the Key of Life   Stevie Wonder

> **"Our parents flipped for that one. That was where the two generations of our family really met, on that album."**
>
> —Heart's Ann Wilson, on *Bridge Over Troubled Water*

albUm

youNg mC's lisT

1. *Rumours* — Fleetwood Mac
2. *Innervisions* — Stevie Wonder
3. *Saturday Night Fever* — Bee Gees

vH1's rosHUmbA's lISt

1. *Parallel Lines* — Blondie
2. *What's Going On* — Marvin Gaye
3. *Dark Side of the Moon* — Pink Floyd

thE besTselliNg albUms frOm thE '7os

1.	*Eagles: Their Greatest Hits 1971–1975*	The Eagles
2.	*The Wall*	Pink Floyd
3.	*Led Zeppelin IV*	Led Zeppelin
4.	*Rumours*	Fleetwood Mac
5.	*Boston*	Boston

Source: RIAA

My List

1.
2.
3.
4.
5.
6.
7.
8.
9.
10.

Best '7os album

●─[beSt '8os

1 "Thriller" — Michael Jackson

2 "Hungry Like the Wolf" — Duran Duran

3 "Sledgehammer" — Peter Gabriel

4 "Take on Me" — A-Ha

5 "Every Breath You Take" — The Police

6 "Don't Come Around Here No More" — Tom Petty and the Heartbreakers

7 "One" — Metallica

8 "Addicted to Love" — Robert Palmer

9 "Express Yourself" — Madonna

10 "Money for Nothing" — Dire Straits

Just Missed
"Pour Some Sugar On Me" — Def Leppard

❝ This was like when art came into it. You not only were selling the product, you not only had the band that you would hose down with the camera, but you now had very arty images and beautiful mystical images, which caused a lot of rot, which caused a lot of terrible videos. ❞

—STEWART COPELAND, ON "EVERY BREATH YOU TAKE"

viDeo

"I'm on the road a lot as a comedian and you need something to masturbate to a lot."

—comedian Robert Schimmel, on "Express Yourself"

stEwart coPelAnd's lIst

1. "Rockit" — Herbie Hancock
2. "Every Breath You Take" — The Police
3. "Legs" — ZZ Top

johN waiTe's liST

1. "When Doves Cry" — Prince
2. "Ashes to Ashes" — David Bowie
3. "Rock the Casbah" — The Clash

fACt

Madonna's video for "Express Yourself," directed by filmmaker David Fincher (*Seven* and *Fight Club*), cost two million dollars. At the time, it was the most expensive video ever made.

My List

1. _____
2. _____
3. _____
4. _____
5. _____
6. _____
7. _____
8. _____
9. _____
10. _____

Best '80s video

beSt '9os

the LiSt

1. **Nirvana**
2. **Pearl Jam**
3. **Dave Matthews Band**
4. **Madonna**
5. **U2**
6. **Garth Brooks**
7. **Alanis Morissette**
8. **Smashing Pumpkins**
9. **Celine Dion**
10. **Shania Twain**

Just Missed
Beck

> **"Madonna you have to admire 'cause she's got the biggest balls in the world."**
> —Patti Smith, VH1 interview

faCt
Between 1991 and 1994 Nirvana released three number one albums and delivered the "grunge" sound of Seattle to the world.

> **"Nirvana cast everything aside and reinvented the genre, and they called it 'alternative rock,' but that's about as metallic as it gets. And it was great."**
> —Dee Snider, VH1 interview

bAnd or artiSt

thE BeStsEllinG uK albUms of tHe '9os

1.	(What's the Story) Morning Glory?	Oasis
2.	Stars	Simply Red
3.	Spice	Spice Girls
4.	Talk on Corners	The Corrs
5.	Jagged Little Pill	Alanis Morissette
6.	Robson & Jerome	Robson & Jerome
7.	The Immaculate Collection	Madonna
8.	Urban Hymns	The Verve
9.	Gold	Abba
10.	Falling Into You	Celine Dion

quiNcy jonEs's liSt

1. Brandy
2. Wyclef Jean
3. Jay-Z

chuCk d'S lIst

1. Wu Tang Clan
2. Rage Against the Machine
3. Tupac Shakur

My List

1 _____
2 _____
3 _____
4 _____
5 _____
6 _____
7 _____
8 _____
9 _____
10 _____

bEst '90s

1	**"Smells Like Teen Spirit"**	Nirvana
2	**"Tears in Heaven"**	Eric Clapton
3	**"Jeremy"**	Pearl Jam
4	**"Enter Sandman"**	Metallica
5	**"Losing My Religion"**	R.E.M.
6	**"You Oughta Know"**	Alanis Morissette
7	**"Crash"**	Dave Matthews Band
8	**"Iris"**	Goo Goo Dolls
9	**"One"**	U2
10	**"Under the Bridge"**	Red Hot Chili Peppers

Just Missed
"Vogue" Madonna

"The '90s were a time of maintenance."
—Robbie Takac of Goo Goo Dolls

soNg

cArnie wiLson's liSt

1. "You Oughta Know"   Alanis Morissette
2. "All I Wanna Do"   Sheryl Crow
3. "Don't Cry"   Seal

duNcan shEik's LiSt

1. "Fake Plastic Trees"   Radiohead
2. "Lover, You Should've Come Over"   Jeff Buckley
3. "Protection"   Massive Attack

faCt
Eric Clapton wrote "Tears in Heaven" as a tribute to his four-and-a-half-year-old son Conor, who died March 20, 1991, after falling out of a window in his mother's 53rd floor Manhattan high-rise apartment.

My List

1 _____
2 _____
3 _____
4 _____
5 _____
6 _____
7 _____
8 _____
9 _____
10 _____

Best '90s Song

●—[beSt '9os

(tie for first place)

1   "Jeremy" — Pearl Jam

"Smells Like Teen Spirit" — Nirvana

2 "Losing My Religion" — R.E.M.

3 "Janie's Got a Gun" — Aerosmith

4 "We Didn't Start the Fire" — Billy Joel

5 "Wicked Game" — Chris Isaak

6 "Sabotage" — Beastie Boys

7 "Living La Vida Loca" — Ricky Martin

8 "Right Now" — Van Halen

9 "Waterfalls" — TLC

10 "Are You Gonna Go My Way?" — Lenny Kravitz

Just Missed
"Ray of Light" — Madonna

amEriCan beAuty'S thoRa BiRch's liSt

1. "Ex-Factor" — Lauryn Hill
2. "Freak on a Leash" — Korn
3. "Waterfalls" — TLC

viDeo

vH1's toP Ten vidEos oF the '9os

1.	"Smells Like Teen Spirit"	Nirvana
2.	"Losing My Religion"	R.E.M.
3.	"Ray of Light"	Madonna
4.	"Sabotage"	Beastie Boys
5.	"Freedom 90"	George Michael
6.	"November Rain"	Guns N' Roses
7.	"Nothing Compares 2 U"	Sinéad O'Connor
8.	"Jeremy"	Pearl Jam
9.	"Wicked Game"	Chris Isaak
10.	"Ironic"	Alanis Morissette

Source: *VH1 Top 90 Videos of the '90s*

fACt
The original budget of $55,000 for the Beastie Boys video for "Sabotage" soared to nearly half a million dollars after director Spike Jonze (*Being John Malkovich*) broke two $200,000 16mm cameras.

Sammy Hagar, former lead singer for Van Halen

My List

1
2
3
4
5
6
7
8
9
10

Best '90s viDeo

27

ƒƒIt's an hour and a half of just brilliance.ƒƒ

—Don Dokken, on *The Joshua Tree*

bESt

1 **Sgt. Pepper's Lonely Hearts Club Band**
The Beatles

-----

2 **Rumours**
Fleetwood Mac

-----

3 **Thriller**
Michael Jackson

-----

4 **Nevermind**
Nirvana

-----

5 **Purple Rain**
Prince

-----

6 **The Joshua Tree**
U2

-----

7 **Are You Experienced?**
Jimi Hendrix Experience

-----

8 **Born to Run**
Bruce Springsteen

-----

9 **Who's Next**
The Who

-----

10 **Bridge Over Troubled Water**
Simon and Garfunkel

Just Missed
Pet Sounds
The Beach Boys

ƒƒI still hear it on the radio today. I'll turn on the alternative radio, I'll turn on hip-hop, I hear it everywhere.ƒƒ

—Everclear's Art Alexakis, on *Sgt. Pepper's Lonely Hearts Club Band*

Heart's Ann Wilson

alBum

"Reinventing the wheel."

—Heart's Nancy Wilson, on
Sgt. Pepper's Lonely Hearts Club Band

tHe beStsEllinG alBums oF all tiMe (u.S. salEs)

1. *Eagles: Their Greatest Hits 1971–1975*	The Eagles	26 million
Thriller	Michael Jackson	
2. *The Wall*	Pink Floyd	23 million
3. *Led Zeppelin IV*	Led Zeppelin	22 million
4. *Greatest Hits Volume I and Volume II*	Billy Joel	20 million

Source: RIAA

aRt alExakIs's lisT

....

1. *Sgt. Pepper's Lonely Hearts Club Band*   The Beatles

2. *It Takes a Nation of Millions to Hold Us Back*   Public Enemy

3. *Physical Graffiti*   Led Zeppelin

fACt

Before Fleetwood Mac entered the studio to record their album, *Rumours*, Stevie Nicks and Lindsy Buckingham broke up, Christine and John McVie divorced, and Mick Fleetwood split from his wife, Jenny.

My List

1 _____
2 _____
3 _____
4 _____
5 _____
6 _____
7 _____
8 _____
9 _____
10 _____

Best Album

●─[seXiest

1. **Ricky Martin**
2. **Elvis Presley**
3. **Britney Spears**
4. **Rick Springfield**
5. **Janet Jackson**
6. **David Cassidy**
7. **'NSYNC**
8. **Mark Wahlberg**
9. **Backstreet Boys**
10. **Spice Girls**

Just Missed
The Monkees

teEn iDol

Ricky Martin's Vital Stats

Born: 12/24/71 Hato Rey, Puerto Rico

Full Name: Enrique Martin Morales Jr.

Sign: Capricorn

Interesting Fact: Ricky was rejected twice by Menudo for being "too small" and "too young" before being accepted into the group after his third audition.

Favorite Film: *The Godfather*

fAct
Britney Spears's nickname is "Bit-Bit" and her favorite song is "Purple Rain."

My List

1
2
3
4
5
6
7
8
9
10

bAnd oR aRtist becoMe a

1. Celine Dion
2. Dave Matthews
3. Lenny Kravitz
4. Mariah Carey
5. Beck
6. Lauryn Hill
7. Nine Inch Nails
8. Sarah McLachlan
9. Smashing Pumpkins
10. Marilyn Manson

fAct

Lenny Kravitz attended high school with future superstars Slash and Nicolas Cage.

moSt LiKely tO
leGend

FACt

Celine Dion is the youngest of fourteen brothers and sisters.

"She's the Bob Marley of the millennium."

—Chuck D, on Lauryn Hill

My List

1. _____
2. _____
3. _____
4. _____
5. _____
6. _____
7. _____
8. _____
9. _____
10. _____

●─[bESt alBu

1 **Sgt. Pepper's Lonely Hearts Club Band** — The Beatles

2 **Dark Side of the Moon** — Pink Floyd

3 **Nevermind** — Nirvana

4 **Houses of the Holy** — Led Zeppelin

5 **Sticky Fingers** — The Rolling Stones

6 **Abraxas** — Santana

7 **License to Ill** — Beastie Boys

8 **Born to Run** — Bruce Springsteen

9 **Strange Days** — The Doors

10 **Elvis Presley** — Elvis Presley

Just Missed
Never Mind the Bollocks — The Sex Pistols

Houses of the Holy

m cOver

vinCe nEil's beSt seX, drUgs & roCk 'n' rOll baNds

1. The Sex Pistols
2. Led Zeppelin
3. The Doors

Ten Album Covers by Andy Warhol

Silk Electric	Diana Ross
Love You Live	The Rolling Stones
Sticky Fingers	The Rolling Stones
The Velvet Underground and Nico	
The Smiths	The Smiths
Rockbird	Deborah Harry
Eat/Kiss Music for the Films	John Cale
Aretha	Aretha Franklin
Emotions in Motion	Billy Squire
The Congregation	Johnny Griffin

My List

1.
2.
3.
4.
5.
6.
7.
8.
9.
10.

Best album cover

o─[beSt '8os

1	*Thriller*	Michael Jackson
2	*Appetite for Destruction*	Guns N' Roses
3	*The Joshua Tree*	U2
4	*Back in Black*	AC/DC
5	*Like a Virgin*	Madonna
6	*Born in the USA*	Bruce Springsteen
7	*Synchronicity*	The Police
8	*Hysteria*	Def Leppard
9	*Kill 'em All*	Metallica
10	*Graceland*	Paul Simon

Just Missed
So — Peter Gabriel

deVo's jErry caSale's lisT

1. *Freedom of Choice* — Devo
2. *Treasure* — The Cocteau Twins
3. *Straight Outta Compton* — N.W.A.

alBum

tHe bEstsellinG albuMs frOm the '80s

1.	*Thriller*	Michael Jackson	25 million
2.	*Greatest Hits Volume I and Volume II*	Billy Joel	21 million
3.	*Back in Black*	AC/DC	16 million
4.	*Appetite for Destruction*	Guns N' Roses	15 million
	Born in the USA	Bruce Springsteen	
5.	*Purple Rain*	Prince	13 million
	Bruce Springsteen & the E Street Band Live 1975–85		

Source: RIAA

FacT

Appetite for Destruction was on *Billboard*'s Top Pop Albums chart for fifty weeks before it hit #1, dethroning Def Leppard's *Hysteria*.

My List

1.
2.
3.
4.
5.
6.
7.
8.
9.
10.

●⊢[bEst '90s

1 ***Nevermind*** — Nirvana

----

2 ***Jagged Little Pill*** — Alanis Morissette

----

3 ***Ten*** — Pearl Jam

----

4 ***BloodSugarSexMagic*** — Red Hot Chili Peppers

----

5 ***Achtung Baby*** — U2

----

6 ***Tragic Kingdom*** — No Doubt

----

7 ***Out of Time*** — R.E.M.

----

8 ***The Miseducation of Lauryn Hill*** — Lauryn Hill

----

9 ***Ray of Light*** — Madonna

----

10 ***CrazySexyCool*** — TLC

Just Missed
Ten Summoner's Tales — Sting

FacT
The Miseducation of Lauryn Hill achieved the distinction of "highest first week sales by a female artist" before going on to capture five Grammy Awards in 1999.

"You could listen to that record start to finish. You don't skip through songs when you listen to *Nevermind*. You listen to it one after another. It's almost like you're cheating yourself if you don't listen to one song off of it."

—Green Day's Billy Joe, VH1 interview

38

alBum

> **"Good lyrics, good singing, good production, good music, good songs."**
>
> —Grace Slick, on *Jagged Little Pill*, VH1 interview

thE bEstselliNg '9os alBums (copies sold)

1.	*Come on Over*	Shania Twain	17 million
	The Bodyguard soundtrack	Whitney Houston	
2.	*Cracked Rear View*	Hootie and the Blowfish	16 million
	Jagged Little Pill	Alanis Morissette	
	No Fences	Garth Brooks	
3.	*Ropin' in the Wind*	Garth Brooks	14 million
4.	*Backstreet Boys*	Backstreet Boys	13 million
	Double Live	Garth Brooks	

Source: RIAA

goO gOo dollS' RoBbie taKac's liSt

1. *Nevermind* — Nirvana
2. *The Bends* — Radiohead
3. *The Downward Spiral* — Nine Inch Nails

My List

1.
2.
3.
4.
5.
6.
7.
8.
9.
10.

Best '9os alBum

39

●—[best arTist

1. Will Smith
2. Cher
3. Bette Midler
4. Mark Wahlberg
5. Jon Bon Jovi
6. Elvis Presley
7. Barbra Streisand
8. Harry Connick Jr.
9. Madonna
10. Kris Kristofferson

Just Missed
David Bowie; Courtney Love

"She's a great singer, a great dresser, a great performer, and she has one name. Cher."

—Lisa Loeb

FacT
Will Smith refused a scholarship to M.I.T. to pursue his music career.

tuRned actOr

"She can probably jump from genre to genre. In other words, act for a while, model, be a rock and roll person, dress up and look sophisticated, in-your-face punk, she probably can do it all."

—Grace Slick, on Courtney Love, VH1 interview

jaCkie colliNs's liSt

1. Mark Wahlberg

2. Madonna

3. Diana Ross

maRio VaN pEEbles'S LiSt

1. Tom Waits

2. Queen Latifah

3. Ice-T

My List

1 _____
2 _____
3 _____
4 _____
5 _____
6 _____
7 _____
8 _____
9 _____
10 _____

Best artist turned Actor

beSt aRtist

1. **Eric Clapton**
2. **Michael Jackson**
3. **Sting**
4. **John Lennon**
5. **Tina Turner**
6. **Paul McCartney**
7. **Phil Collins**
8. **Janis Joplin**
9. **Don Henley**
10. **Annie Lennox**

Just Missed
Stevie Nicks

fAcT
Before launching his solo career, Eric Clapton was a member of John Mayall's Bluesbreakers, The Yardbirds, Cream, Blind Faith, and Derek and the Dominoes.

"When he went solo he changed the industry."

—Snoop Dogg, on Michael Jackson

wHo weNT sOlo

toP fiVe arTists wHo leFt tOp grOups to becOme moRe sucCesful

1. Michael Jackson
2. Eric Clapton
3. Phil Collins
4. Ozzy Osbourne
5. Lionel Richie

Source: RIAA

paT bOone's liSt

1. Diana Ross
2. Paul McCartney
3. Phil Collins

snOop doGg's lIst

1. Michael Jackson
2. Curtis Mayfield
3. Smokey Robinson

My List

1.
2.
3.
4.
5.
6.
7.
8.
9.
10.

beSt roCk

		Arrested for:
1	**Jim Morrison**	public indecency
2	**Ozzy Osbourne**	urinating on the Alamo
3	**Axl Rose**	assault
4	**Tommy Lee**	assault
5	**Alice Cooper**	never arrested
6	**Steven Tyler**	never arrested
7	**Sid Vicious**	murder
8	**Elvis Presley**	never arrested
9	**Keith Moon**	manslaughter
10	**Mick Jagger**	drug possession

Just Missed
Marilyn Manson; David Lee Roth; Johnny Rotten

❝He was thrown out of Black Sabbath for drug use. Do you know how many drugs you have to do to have the band saying 'I think Ozzy's got a problem?'❞

— comic Adam Ferrera

7 arTists deAd aT 27

1. Jim Morrison
2. Kurt Cobain
3. Janis Joplin
4. Nick Drake
5. Jimi Hendrix
6. Brian Jones
7. Robert Johnson

'n' rOll baD bOy

geOrge THorogood's liSt

1. Bob Dylan
2. Paul McCartney
3. Keith Richards

> **"First** of all, Mick Jagger, who everybody thinks and calls a true bad boy, *his* idol is Keith Richards.**"**
>
> —George Thorogood

Rob Zombie

roB zoMbie'S lisT

1. G. G. Allin
2. Ozzy Osbourne
3. Jerry Lee Lewis

leIf gaRrett's lIst

1. Keith Richards
2. Keith Moon
3. Sid Vicious

> **"He was the baddest boy in the world."**
>
> —Leif Garrett, on Sid Vicious

My List

1
2
3
4
5
6
7
8
9
10

beSt roCk

1. Janis Joplin
2. Courtney Love
3. Madonna
4. Grace Slick
5. Joan Jett
6. Stevie Nicks
7. Cher
8. Wendy O. Williams
9. Debbie Harry
10. Lita Ford

Just Missed
Fiona Apple; Chrissie Hynde

"She's like the sexiest chick you don't want to have sex with."

—Ice-T, on Wendy O. Williams

'n' rOll baD giRL

poIson's c.C. devIlle's LIst

1. Tina Turner
2. Carly Simon
3. Marianne Faithfull

> **"She's the kind of girl you could get drunk with and then when we're done and the alcohol is gone, you could go out and rob a liquor store."**
>
> —comic Christopher Titus, on Courtney Love

fAcT
Janis Joplin's will called for 200 of her friends to throw a party in her memory at her favorite pub in San Anselma, California, at a cost of $2,500.

My List

1
2
3
4
5
6
7
8
9
10

best rOCk 'n roll baD Grl

beSt boy

1. **Duran Duran**

2. **The Beach Boys**

3. **The Monkees**

4. **The Jackson 5**

5. **Backstreet Boys**

6. **'NSYNC**

7. **Boyz II Men**

8. **New Kids on the Block**

9. **Wham**

10. **Hanson**

Just Missed
2Gether

faCT
In April of 2000, 'NSYNC's *No Strings Attached* became the first single-disc album to be certified for U.S. sales of 7 million copies in its initial RIAA audit, breaking a record set in 1993 by *The Bodyguard* soundtrack, which was certified at 6 million copies in its first audit.
Source: RIAA

"I'm not saying they're gay, but they're not on the front streets."
— comic Greg Fitzsimmons, on Backstreet Boys

baNd or groUp

"My earliest memory of the Jackson 5 is all the girls at school picked the Jackson they loved and that was their boyfriend. I picked Marlon because I knew there wasn't as much competition for him."

—Rupaul, VH1 interview

juLio iGlesias jr.'S list

1. The Jackson 5
2. New Kids on the Block
3. 'NSYNC

DeboRah giBson's LiSt

1. The Beatles
2. Bros
3. Backstreet Boys

"They are the boy band of the new generation."

—Deborah Gibson, on Backstreet Boys

My List

1. _____
2. _____
3. _____
4. _____
5. _____
6. _____
7. _____
8. _____
9. _____
10. _____

●─[bEst coMe

1 Santana

2 Aerosmith

3 Tina Turner

4 Cher

5 Eric Clapton

6 Meat Loaf

7 Elvis Presley

8 Bee Gees

9 Brian Setzer

10 Bonnie Raitt

Just Missed
Heart

> **facT**
> At the 2000 Grammy Awards, Santana's #1 album *Supernatural* won eight Grammy awards, tieing the world record held by Michael Jackson for most Grammies awarded to an album.

"I don't think he's a comeback. I think he's been here all along; but he's embraced a new audience and we in the business say it's a comeback because if the artist is annoyed by it you have to say it."
—Three Dog Night's Chuck Negron, on Santana

bAck BaNd or artiSt

toMmy shaW's LIst

1. Elvis Presley
2. Aerosmith
3. KISS

> **"They put the makeup on and froze themselves in time, which most us can't do."**
>
> —Styx's Tommy Shaw, on KISS

chuCk NeGron's liSt

1. Fleetwood Mac
2. Brian Setzer
3. Ricky Martin

fAcT

In 1977 Meat Loaf took the world by storm with *Bat Out of Hell* (7 million copies sold in the U.S.), then all but disappeared for more than ten years. In 1993 he released *Bat Out of Hell II: Back Into Hell* which quickly rose to #1 on the Album Chart and sold 10 million copies worldwide in its first three months of release.

My List

1
2
3
4
5
6
7
8
9
10

beSt coVer

1 **"All Along the Watchtower"** — Jimi Hendrix (Bob Dylan)

2 **"Respect"** — Aretha Franklin (Otis Redding)

3 **"I Will Always Love You"** — Whitney Houston (Dolly Parton)

4 **"Twist and Shout"** — The Beatles (The Isley Brothers)

5 **"I Shot the Sheriff"** — Eric Clapton (Bob Marley)

6 **"Walk This Way"** — Run-D.M.C. with Aerosmith (Aerosmith)

7 **"Proud Mary"** — Ike and Tina Turner (Creedence Clearwater Revival)

8 **"Killing Me Softly"** — The Fugees (Roberta Flack)

9 **"The Man Who Sold the World"** — Nirvana (David Bowie)

10 **"Nothing Compares 2 U"** — Sinéad O'Connor (Prince)

Just Missed
"Have I Told You Lately" — Rod Stewart (Van Morrison)

soNg

sevEn soNgs covEred by boB dylAn

1.	"Alabama Getaway"	The Grateful Dead
2.	"Big Yellow Taxi"	Joni Mitchell
3.	"The Boxer"	Simon and Garfunkel
4.	"Can't Help Falling in Love"	Elvis Presley
5.	"Ring of Fire"	Johnny Cash
6.	"Lonesome Town"	Ricky Nelson
7.	"Dancing in the Dark"*	Bruce Springsteen

*Performed only once live at the legendary Toad's Place show in New Haven, Connecticut, January 12, 1990.

" Growing up when I grew up it wasn't really considered cool to listen to rock and roll. You had to listen to Motown or Al Green; but I had some rock and roll in my house and would never play it when my friends were around. I play it, my mom plays it, and you know, me and my mom sing it together. You know some Rolling Stones, Three Dog Night, groups like that, Fleetwood Mac and that kinda stuff. So Run-D.M.C. made it cool, you know, to listen to rock and roll. And it was cool and then a lot of black kids came out of the closet pretty much. **"**

—COOLIO

My List

1. _____
2. _____
3. _____
4. _____
5. _____
6. _____
7. _____
8. _____
9. _____
10. _____

bEst covEr soNg

53

bESt dAn

1	**"I Will Survive"**	Gloria Gaynor
2	**"Stayin' Alive"**	Bee Gees
3	**"YMCA"**	The Village People
4	**"Vogue"**	Madonna
5	**"The Twist"**	Chubby Checker
6	**"Last Dance"**	Donna Summer
7	**"Get Down Tonight"**	KC and the Sunshine Band
8	**"Respect"**	Aretha Franklin
9	**"Louie Louie"**	The Kingsmen
10	**"Don't Stop Till You Get Enough"**	Michael Jackson

Just Missed
"Gonna Make You Sweat"　　　　　C&C Music Factory

---

moSt spUn tAbles bY a sinGle DJ

1. Cut La Roc (eight tables)
2. DJ Trixta (six tables)

Source: *Guinness World Records 2000*

> **"It seemed like the whole world was doing the Twist. It taught a lot of uptight people how to move their bodies finally."**
>
> —The B-52s' Fred Schneider, VH1 interview

ce soNg

toNi baSil's lisT

1. "The Power" — Snap!
2. "Land of a Thousand Dances" — Wilson Pickett
3. "I Feel for You" — Chaka Khan

talK SOup's haL SPark's lIst

1. "Stayin' Alive" — Bee Gees
2. "Footloose" — Kenny Loggins
3. "We Got the Beat" — The Go-Gos

My List

1. _____
2. _____
3. _____
4. _____
5. _____
6. _____
7. _____
8. _____
9. _____
10. _____

Best dAnce soNg

⊶[beST diS

1	**"Stayin' Alive"**	Bee Gees
2	**"I Will Survive"**	Gloria Gaynor
3	**"YMCA"**	The Village People
4	**"Dancing Queen"**	Abba
5	**"Play That Funky Music"**	Wild Cherry
6	**"That's the Way (I Like It)"**	KC and the Sunshine Band
7	**"Heart of Glass"**	Blondie
8	**"Funkytown"**	Lipps, Inc.
9	**"Le Freak"**	Chic
10	**"Disco Inferno"**	The Tramps

Just Missed
"Hot Stuff"   Donna Summer

> **❝It's one of those songs that makes you feel like you're under the ball again and you're dancing in the middle of a dancefloor.❞**
>
> —Evelyn Champagne King, on "Dancing Queen," VH1 interview

co soNg

Studio 54 Regulars

Andy Warhol

Bianca Jagger

Grace Jones

Truman Capote

Liza Minnelli

Jerry Hall

Calvin Klein

Eartha Kitt

meRediTh brOoks's lISt

1. "Love to Love You Baby" Donna Summer
2. "I Will Survive" Gloria Gaynor
3. "Lady Marmalade" LaBelle

My List

1
2
3
4
5
6
7
8
9
10

Best disco song

bEst feM

1. **Aretha Franklin**
2. **Madonna**
3. **Janis Joplin**
4. **Stevie Nicks**
5. **Tina Turner**
6. **Celine Dion**
7. **Billie Holiday**
8. **Barbra Streisand**
9. **Whitney Houston**
10. **Annie Lennox**

Just Missed
Cher

> **"She does a version of 'Drown in My Own Tears.' It's pretty hard to beat Ray Charles on a song he did first. But she sort of manages that."**
>
> —Elvis Costello, on Aretha Franklin, VH1 interview

ale siNger

"She sang with such passion, from so far down deep inside her, that she just moves you, just breaks your heart like no one."

—Melissa Etheridge, on Janis Joplin, VH1 interview

shEila e.'s liSt

1. Celine Dion
2. CeCe Winans
3. Patti Labelle

"I like her because she takes all kinds of chances. She's brave. She's got a terrific kind of 'screw you' attitude. 'I'm gonna do it this way.' And you tend to follow along and admire it."

— Liza Minnelli, on Madonna, VH1 interview

My List

1. _____
2. _____
3. _____
4. _____
5. _____
6. _____
7. _____
8. _____
9. _____
10. _____

Best feMale SiNgeR

●─[beSt frOnt

1	**Stevie Nicks**	Fleetwood Mac
2	**Annie Lennox**	Eurythmics
3	**Janis Joplin**	Big Brother and the Holding Company
4	**Debbie Harry**	Blondie
5	**Gwen Stefani**	No Doubt
6	**Diana Ross**	The Supremes
7	**Chrissie Hynde**	The Pretenders
8	**Ann Wilson**	Heart
9	**Gloria Estefan**	Miami Sound Machine
10	**Courtney Love**	Hole

Just Missed
Grace Slick   Jefferson Airplane

"She's just one of the best front people of all time. She's so hot, too."

—Adam Duritz, on Chrissie Hynde, VH1 interview

woMan

"When Janis Joplin started singing, she was performing sex to 20,000 people."

—Meat Loaf

Meat Loaf

actRess hOlly robiNson's LIst

1. Chaka Khan   Rufus
2. Debbie Harry   Blondie
3. Lauryn Hill   The Fugees

My List

1
2
3
4
5
6
7
8
9
10

Best front woMan

beSt frOnt

1	**Jim Morrison**	The Doors
2	**Freddie Mercury**	Queen
3	**Bono**	U2
4	**David Lee Roth**	Van Halen
5	**Kurt Cobain**	Nirvana
6	**Steven Tyler**	Aerosmith
7	**Anthony Kiedis**	Red Hot Chili Peppers
8	**Mick Jagger**	The Rolling Stones
9	**Sting**	The Police
10	**James Hetfield**	Metallica

Just Missed
Michael Jackson   The Jackson 5

"He looks great in leather pants."
—*ER*'s Alex Kingston, on Bono

man

alEx kinGston's LiSt

1. Freddie Mercury

2. Bono

3. Mick Jagger

Minnie Driver

"I kind of enjoy David Lee Roth in Spandex. There's something enticing about that."

—Sheryl Crow, VH1 interview

My List

1
2
3
4
5
6
7
8
9
10

Best front MAn

beSt giRL

1. **The Supremes**
2. **The Go-Gos**
3. **TLC**
4. **The Bangles**
5. **The Dixie Chicks**
6. **En Vogue**
7. **Salt-n-Pepa**
8. **The Pointer Sisters**
9. **Indigo Girls**
10. **Bananarama**

Just Missed
The Runaways

> "I'm very grateful for groups like the Supremes that have gone ahead of us because they have helped pave the road and make it easier for female artists today."
>
> —En Vogue's Cindy Herron

baNd or groUp

FaCT
The Supremes are the only girl group to have had five straight number one singles.

wiLd orChid's, stAcy fergUson's lIst

1. The Supremes
2. Heart
3. En Vogue

wRiter IlEne rosenZweig's liSt

1. Salt-n-Pepa
2. The Shangri-Las
3. The Ronettes

My List

1
2
3
4
5
6
7
8
9
10

best girL Band or group

65

beSt hAir

1. **Bon Jovi**
2. **Guns N' Roses**
3. **Poison**
4. **Motley Crüe**
5. **KISS**
6. **Def Leppard**
7. **Twisted Sister**
8. **Whitesnake**
9. **Cinderella**
10. **Skid Row**

Just Missed
Queensryche

haiRband essEntials

1. Hairspray
2. Spandex pants
3. Tattoos
4. Stripper or model girlfriends
5. Eyeliner
6. Fingernail polish
7. Scarves! Scarves! Scarves!

baNd

kiP winGEr's lisT

1. Def Leppard
2. KISS
3. ZZ Top

ER's Gloria Reuben

My List

1 _____
2 _____
3 _____
4 _____
5 _____
6 _____
7 _____
8 _____
9 _____
10 _____

Best har band

○─[beST hEa

1. **Metallica**
2. **Led Zeppelin**
3. **AC/DC**
4. **KISS**
5. **Black Sabbath**
6. **Def Leppard**
7. **Motley Crüe**
8. **Rage Against the Machine**
9. **Limp Bizkit**
10. **Korn**

Just Missed
Tool; Spinal Tap

> ❝I was a little kid in New Jersey, and rock and roll was for grownups, and all of a sudden one day, KISS came out with makeup and it was rock and roll for the mainstream, and they were Jewish. I mean my mom was so into that. I was like, 'Mom, they spit blood and they worship the devil.' 'Yeah, but they're Jewish guys, it's all right.'❞
>
> — comic, Jeff Ross

vy meTal baNd

roB halfOrd's lIst

1. Black Sabbath
2. Metallica
3. Rage Against the Machine

"Thinking man's metal."
—Rob Halford, on Metallica

JUlie strAin's lisT

1. Poison
2. Judas Priest
3. KISS

"Black Sabbath has always been number one for me, always number one. Everything starts from an original source or date and they're the originators of heavy metal music."
—Judas Priest's Rob Halford

My List

1. _____
2. _____
3. _____
4. _____
5. _____
6. _____
7. _____
8. _____
9. _____
10. _____

⊶[bEst leAd

① Jimi Hendrix

② Eric Clapton

③ Jimmy Page

④ Eddie Van Halen

⑤ Carlos Santana

⑥ Stevie Ray Vaughan

⑦ Kirk Hammett

⑧ Randy Rhoads

⑨ B.B. King

⑩ Angus Young

Just Missed
George Harrison

❝ This guy was an extraordinary musician. I'd never seen the guitar played that way. It was mind-blowing, I mean really mind-blowing. Another one of those seminal experiences that informed the rest of your life, you know, 'That's what I want to do. I wanna be a pop star and be able to play as well as that.' Of course, I never ever got to play as well as that, but the *desire* to is something that is still with me. ❞

—Sting, on Jimi Hendrix, VH1 interview

guitaRist

matthEw SWeet's lIst

1. Jimi Hendrix

2. James Burton

3. Peter Green

"When you're a girl who plays guitar, people expect you to play pretty, and I was always trying to push away pretty and, you know, come up with stuff that was more interesting and more dissonant and more left-of-center and offbeat, like Jimmy Page."

—Heart's Nancy Wilson,
VH1 interview

bevErly HilLs 90210's IaN zieRing's LiSt

1. Jimi Hendrix

2. Jimmy Page

3. Mark Knopfler

My List

1
2
3
4
5
6
7
8
9
10

Best leaD GutARist

●—[beST LiVe

1 Aerosmith

2 Madonna

3 The Rolling Stones

4 Bruce Springsteen

5 U2

6 Red Hot Chili Peppers

7 Dave Matthews Band

8 Garth Brooks

9 Tina Turner

10 The Who

Just Missed
Michael Jackson

Steve Harwell

"We opened a few shows for U2 and I was not a big U2 fan. But after I actually walked out and saw their Pop Mart tour, their show, it's overwhelming. "

—Smash Mouth's Steve Harwell, VH1 interview

peRFormer

❝I tried to get how to behave on a stage from Mick Jagger. In the sense that you walk on a stage and you own it, and if you don't, the audience is gonna know it.❞

—Grace Slick, VH1 interview

riTa rudnEr's lisT

1. Bruce Springsteen

2. Tom Jones

3. Tina Turner

The Best Shows I've Seen

1 _____
2 _____
3 _____
4 _____
5 _____
6 _____
7 _____
8 _____
9 _____
10 _____

best Live PeRfoRMer

bEst loVe

1	**"Can't Help Falling in Love"**	Elvis Presley
2	**"Wonderful Tonight"**	Eric Clapton
3	**"(Everything I Do) I Do It for You"**	Bryan Adams
4	**"Unchained Melody"**	The Righteous Brothers
5	**"My Heart Will Go On"**	Celine Dion
6	**"I Will Always Love You"**	Whitney Houston
7	**"Your Song"**	Elton John
8	**"Something"**	The Beatles
9	**"Endless Love"**	Diana Ross and Lionel Richie
10	**"When a Man Loves a Woman"**	Percy Sledge

Just Missed
"Crazy" — Patsy Cline

MC Hammer

FaCT

"Can't Help Falling in Love" peaked at #2 on the *Billboard* Top 40 in 1962, but hit #1 when UB40 released their reggae version in the summer of 1993. It stayed on top for seven weeks.

74

soNg

thE fiVe beAtles sonGs covEred by elVis preSley

1. "Something"

2. "Lady Madonna"

3. "Get Back"

4. "Hey Jude"

5. "Let It Be"

FaCT

"(Everything I Do) I Do It for You" had a seven-week run at #1 in the U.S. and a sixteen-week run at #1 in the U.K.

"That song can be used to mark a memory in someone's life, a relationship, a prom, a wedding, whatever. Elton's done that to us time and time and time again for thirty years."

—Jon Bon Jovi, on "Your Song,"
VH1 interview

My List

1
2
3
4
5
6
7
8
9
10

Best love song

bEst malE

1 Freddie Mercury

2 John Lennon

3 Elvis Presley

4 Sting

5 Elton John

6 Jim Morrison

7 Paul McCartney

8 Bono

9 Marvin Gaye

10 Robert Plant

Just Missed
Michael Jackson

"People like Michael [Jackson] come along once in history."
—Teddy Pendergrass, VH1 interview

"People have actually told me they've had babies to Marvin Gaye."
—R. Kelly

siNger

toP fiVe-sElling miChael jAckson aLbums woRldwide

1.	*Thriller*	51 million
2.	*History: Past, Present, Future, Book 1*	30 million
3.	*Dangerous*	27 million
4.	*Bad*	25 million
5.	*Off the Wall*	15 million

Source: RIAA

❝John Lennon was the original punk rocker.❞

—*Ally McBeal's* Gil Bellows

My List

1.
2.
3.
4.
5.
6.
7.
8.
9.
10.

Best mae siNger

—[bEst mAle

1 Elvis Presley

2 Elton John

3 Jimi Hendrix

4 John Lennon

5 Sting

6 Eric Clapton

7 Bruce Springsteen

8 David Bowie

9 Prince

10 Bob Dylan

Just Missed
Garth Brooks; Paul McCartney

> **"I'm not worthy to carry his guitar case. He stands alone. He doesn't have a George Harrison or Ringo Starr to pal out with. He's all alone and he's done it all in rock. He's like Gary Cooper in *High Noon,* he stands alone."**
>
> **—George Thorogood, on Bob Dylan**

Laura San Giacomo

sOlo aRtist

bestsElling AlBums bY a maLe sOlo ARtist

		(U.S. Sales)
1. *Thriller*	Michael Jackson	25 million
2. *Greatest Hits Volume I and Volume II*		
	Billy Joel	20 million
3. *No Fences*	Garth Brooks	16 million
4. *Born in the USA*	Bruce Springsteen	15 million
Greatest Hits	Elton John	

Source: RIAA

tyrEse's LiSt

1. R. Kelly
2. Bobby Brown
3. Garth Brooks

edDie monEy's lisT

1. James Brown
2. Eddie Money
3. Rod Stewart

My List

1
2
3
4
5
6
7
8
9
10

beSt moV

1	**Saturday Night Fever**
2	**Grease**
3	**Purple Rain**
4	**Forrest Gump**
5	**Dirty Dancing**
6	**Footloose**
7	**Pulp Fiction**
8	**The Breakfast Club**
9	**The Big Chill**
10	**Yellow Submarine**

Just Missed

The Song Remains the Same

❝You love it or you hate it. This album is the most influential album of the time. I can count eleven or twelve songs off this record that everyone knows.❞

—Young MC, on *Saturday Night Fever*

ie soUndtraCk

thE beStselliNg soUndtRacks oF alL tiMe

1.	*The Bodyguard*	16 million
2.	*Saturday Night Fever*	15 million
3.	*Purple Rain*	13 million
4.	*Forrest Gump*	12 million
5.	*Dirty Dancing* and *Titanic*	11 million (tie)
6.	*The Lion King*	10 million
7.	*Top Gun*	9 million
8.	*Grease* and *Footloose*	8 million (tie)
9.	*Waiting to Exhale*	7 million

Source: *Billboard*

diRector aMy heCkerling's lIst

1. *West Side Story*
2. *American Graffiti*
3. *Saturday Night Fever*

My List

1. _____
2. _____
3. _____
4. _____
5. _____
6. _____
7. _____
8. _____
9. _____
10. _____

Best Movie Soundtrack

●─[bESt moV

1	"Stayin' Alive"	*Saturday Night Fever*
2	"A Hard Day's Night"	*A Hard Day's Night*
3	"Mrs. Robinson"	*The Graduate*
4	"Purple Rain"	*Purple Rain*
5	"My Heart Will Go On"	*Titanic*
6	"I Don't Wanna Miss a Thing"	*Armaggedon*
7	"Footloose"	*Footloose*
8	"Danger Zone"	*Top Gun*
9	"I Will Always Love You"	*The Bodyguard*
10	"The Time of My Life"	*Dirty Dancing*

Just Missed
"Circle of Life"   *The Lion King*

viVica A. fOx's liSt

1. "Call Me"   *American Gigolo*
2. "Beautiful Stranger"   *Austin Powers*
3. "Don't Let Go"   *Set It Off*

FaCT
Paul Simon was commissioned by Mike Nichols to score the entire film of *The Graduate*. "Mrs. Robinson" was the only *new* piece he wrote that made it into the film.

ie thEme soNg

jUst shOot mE's, enRico colAntoni's liST

1. "Don't You (Forget About Me)" *The Breakfast Club*

2. "Up Where We Belong" *An Officer and a Gentleman*

3. "La Bamba" *La Bamba*

My List

1
2
3
4
5
6
7
8
9
10

best movie theme song

O-[beSt muS

the List

1 "Thriller" — Michael Jackson

2 "Smells Like Teen Spirit" — Nirvana

3 "Jeremy" — Pearl Jam

4 "Sledgehammer" — Peter Gabriel

5 "Hungry Like the Wolf" — Duran Duran

6 "Take On Me" — A-Ha

7 "Losing My Religion" — R.E.M.

8 "Don't Come Around Here No More" — Tom Petty and the Heartbreakers

9 "Vogue" — Madonna

10 "Addicted to Love" — Robert Palmer

Just Missed
"Money for Nothing" — Dire Straits

faCT

"Hungry Like the Wolf" was the first video shot on film.

ic viDeo

dyAn caNnon's LiSt

1. "Music of My Heart"   'NSYNC with Gloria Estefan
2. "Beat It"   Michael Jackson
3. "Bring Me a Higher Love"   Steve Winwood

thE b-52s' kAte pieRson's lIst

1. "Human Behavior"   Bjork
2. "Mama Said Knock You Out"   LL Cool J
3. "Nothing Compares 2 U"   Sinéad O'Connor

My List

1.
2.
3.
4.
5.
6.
7.
8.
9.
10.

Best music viDeo

beSt neW

the LiSt

1	**Duran Duran**
2	**The Police**
3	**INXS**
4	**Depeche Mode**
5	**Eurythmics**
6	**The Cure**
7	**The B-52s**
8	**Talking Heads**
9	**The Cars**
10	**Culture Club**

Just Missed
Devo

> ❝ The B-52s are inherently artistic, interesting people. Their world is a very artistic world. Debbie Harry and David Bowie and artists like that, whose lives revolve around a certain sort of aesthetic, that's what keeps them around. They always have something interesting to say because they have interesting forces around them to pull from. ❞
>
> —Nile Rodgers, VH1 interview

wAve baNd or Artist

thOmas doLby's liSt

1. Talking Heads
2. Psychedelic Furs
3. XTC

❝They had a great drummer, a really melodic guitar player, a great singer and bass player and songwriter, and they made you feel like going into the '80s that anything was possible musically.❞

—Men at Work's Colin Hay, on the Police

loVe aNd rocKets's dAniEl aSh's lisT

1. Pet Shop Boys
2. New Order
3. Devo

My List

1. _____
2. _____
3. _____
4. _____
5. _____
6. _____
7. _____
8. _____
9. _____
10. _____

bEst piAno/

1. **Elton John**
2. **Billy Joel**
3. **Stevie Wonder**
4. **Jerry Lee Lewis**
5. **Harry Connick Jr.**
6. **Ray Charles**
7. **Tori Amos**
8. **Little Richard**
9. **Ray Manzarek (The Doors)**
10. **Bruce Hornsby**

Just Missed
Sarah McLachlan

> **"Ray Charles made country music understandable for people who lived in New York City."**
>
> —Billy Joel, VH1 interview

keyBoard plAyer

❝He was probably the hardest rocker of the fifties.❞

—Brian Wilson, on Little Richard, VH1 interview

FaCT

On October 17, 2000, George Michael purchased the Steinway piano on which John Lennon composed "Imagine." His bid of approximately $2.1 million beat out Robbie Williams and Liam and Noel Gallagher.

❝I think that he would have been Elvis except that he was so insane he threw his career away.❞

—Rob Zombie,
on Jerry Lee Lewis

Rob Zombie

My List

1
2
3
4
5
6
7
8
9
10

best piano/keyBoard plAyer

bESt pOp

1	*Thriller*	Michael Jackson
2	*Meet the Beatles*	The Beatles
3	*Rumours*	Fleetwood Mac
4	*Purple Rain*	Prince
	Like a Virgin	Madonna
5	*Bat Out of Hell*	Meat Loaf
6	*Saturday Night Fever*	Bee Gees
7	*Goodbye Yellow Brick Road*	Elton John
8	*Frampton Comes Alive*	Peter Frampton
9	*Escape*	Journey
10	*Millennium*	Backstreet Boys

Just Missed
Faith   George Michael

"He's a very smart cookie, Michael. He knows what he wants; he knows exactly what he's doing. I have nothing but admiration for him."

—Elton John, on Michael Jackson, VH1 interview

FaCT
Michael Jackson's *Thriller* has sold upwards of 47 million copies to date, worldwide, which is the most copies sold by any single album in the history of popular music.

aLBum

zaC haNson's liSt

1. *Thriller*   Michael Jackson
2. *Pet Sounds*   The Beach Boys
3. *August and Everything After*   Counting Crows

tayLor hanSon's LIst

1. *Eagles: Their Greatest Hits 1971-75*
2. *Déjà Vu*   Crosby, Stills, Nash and Young
3. *The Joshua Tree*   U2

isAac hansOn's lisT

1. *Graceland*   Paul Simon
2. *River of Dreams*   Billy Joel
3. *Rubber Soul*   The Beatles

My List

1 _____
2 _____
3 _____
4 _____
5 _____
6 _____
7 _____
8 _____
9 _____
10 _____

91

Best Pop alBum

best poP

1 The Beatles

2 Duran Duran

3 The Eagles

4 Fleetwood Mac

5 The Police

6 Bon Jovi

7 The Beach Boys

8 Bee Gees

9 Abba

10 The Jackson 5

Just Missed
Blondie

> **"If anybody were gonna tell me that there are aliens walking on the Earth, who do you think they are? I'd say, well, the Beatles for sure, because nobody could write that many good songs without being supernatural."**
>
> —Alice Cooper, VH1 interview

gRoup

voNda shePard's liSt

1. The Beatles
2. Aretha Franklin
3. Carole King

"They made the marriage of black and white. They put it right in the middle and said, 'Hey, we're funky, we're doing it.' And it worked."

—Donna Summer, on the Bee Gees, VH1 interview

grOups witH mOst golD alBums	
1. The Beatles	40
2. The Rolling Stones	38
3. KISS	23
4. Alabama Rush	22
5. Aerosmith Chicago	21

Source: RIAA

My List

1.
2.
3.
4.
5.
6.
7.
8.
9.
10.

Best Pop grOup

93

⊶[bEst POp

1 "I Want to Hold Your Hand" — The Beatles

2 "California Dreamin'" — The Mamas and the Papas

3 "Good Vibrations" — The Beach Boys

4 "When Doves Cry" — Prince

5 "Stayin' Alive" — Bee Gees

6 "I Will Survive" — Gloria Gaynor

7 "Billie Jean" — Michael Jackson

8 "Dancing Queen" — Abba

9 "Iris" — Goo Goo Dolls

10 "Like a Virgin" — Madonna

Just Missed (tied)

"Girls Just Wanna Have Fun" — Cyndi Lauper

"You're the One That I Want" — John Travolta and Olivia Newton-John

soNg

loU beGa's lIst

1. "Is This Love?" — Bob Marley
2. "I Got You" — James Brown
3. "Billie Jean" — Michael Jackson

tOp-SElling siNgles of aLL tiMe (U.S.)

1. "Candle in the Wind" (1997)	Elton John	11 million
2. (six tied for second place)		
"I Will Always Love You"	Whitney Houston	4 million
"Macarena"	Los Del Rio	
"We Are the World"	USA for Africa	
"Whoomp (There It Is)"	Tag Team	
"Hey Jude"	The Beatles	
"Hound Dog"/"Don't Be Cruel"	Elvis Presley	

Source: *Billboard*

Brian McKnight's List

1. "I Believe I Can Fly" — R. Kelly
2. "Endless Love" Lionel Richie and Diana Ross
3. "I Want to Hold Your Hand" The Beatles

My List

1
2
3
4
5
6
7
8
9
10

Best Pop song

95

beSt r&b

1. **Aretha Franklin**

2. **Marvin Gaye**

3. **Stevie Wonder**

4. **Tina Turner**

5. **James Brown**

6. **Otis Redding**

7. **Ray Charles**

8. **Al Green**

9. **Whitney Houston**

10. **Lionel Richie**

Just Missed
Luther Vandross

> **"He goes down as an R&B song himself."**
> —producer Dallas Austin, on Al Green

> **"This guy is somebody who is so smooth he'll slice your toast for you and put butter on it."**
> —Dennis Franz, on Al Green

aRtist

❝I was raised with James. We was raised up from kids together in Macon, Georgia. We used to play together when we was kids. He used to beat me when we was kids.❞

—Little Richard, on James Brown

acTress jaiMe prEssly's LisT

1. Aretha Franklin
2. Tina Turner
3. Lauryn Hill

❝He should be remembered for being the great artist he was.❞

—Colin Hay, on Marvin Gaye

LOu diaMond pHillips's LIst

1. Aretha Franklin
2. B.B. King
3. Stevie Wonder

My List

1
2
3
4
5
6
7
8
9
10

97

Best R&b aRtists

○─[beST rAp

1 Will Smith

2 Beastie Boys

3 Run-D.M.C.

4 LL Cool J

5 Eminem

6 Salt-n-Pepa;
Queen Latifah

7 Tupac Shakur

8 Public Enemy

9 Ice-T

10 The Fugees

Just Missed
Snoop Doggy Dogg

FacT
Before finding their
true calling as a hip-hop
group, the Beastie Boys
were a punk rock band who
released an EP titled
Polly Wog Stew.

**❝He came out two years before
me and I wanted to be him.❞**

—Heavy D, on LL Cool J

groUp or arTist

heAvy d'S liSt

1. Slick Rick
2. Jay-Z
3. LL Cool J

b-REal's lISt

1. KRS-One
2. Busta Rhymes
3. Eminem

"The thing about LL is he's always been able to evolve with the times and do things that his fans will appreciate at the time, you know what I mean? He's one of a few handfuls that have been able to carry his career on past ten years."

—B-Real from Cypress Hill

My List

1
2
3
4
5
6
7
8
9
10

⊶[bESt roCk

1. **Grease**

2. **Rocky Horror Picture Show**

3. **A Hard Day's Night**

4. **Dirty Dancing**

5. **Purple Rain**

6. **The Wall**

7. **The Doors**

8. **This Is Spinal Tap**

9. **Footloose**

10. **Tommy**

Just Missed
Woodstock

"Let me tell you something, right now! When that chick dressed up in them leathers in *Grease* and she walked out and put that cigarette butt out, that broad was sexy!"

—Meat Loaf, on Olivia Newton-John

aNd rOll fiIM

shErilyn FEnn's liSt

1. *Spice World*
2. *Purple Rain*
3. *Tommy*

leOnard maLtin's lisT

1. *Jailhouse Rock*
2. *A Hard Day's Night*
3. *Tommy*

jeFf conAway's LiSt

1. *Grease*
2. *Yellow Submarine*
3. *Woodstock*

My List

1	
2	
3	
4	
5	
6	
7	
8	
9	
10	

bESt roCk

"At some point in an artist's career, they make an album that is that transitional, pivotal record. For me, _Revolver_ is that record."

—Hootie & the Blowfish's Mark Bryan

1	*Dark Side of the Moon*	Pink Floyd
2	*Led Zeppelin II*	Led Zeppelin
3	*Back in Black*	AC/DC
4	*Appetite for Destruction*	Guns N' Roses
5	*Nevermind*	Nirvana
6	*The Doors*	The Doors
7	*Revolver*	The Beatles
8	*The Joshua Tree*	U2
9	*Are You Experienced?*	Jimi Hendrix Experience
10	*Born to Run*	Bruce Springsteen

Just Missed
Ten   Pearl Jam

"That was the cool thing about them too, you know, at a real safe period in rock and roll, and all of a sudden Guns came out and were like, 'We don't care.'"

—Megadeth's David Elfson, on Guns N' Roses

alBUm

daRius ruCker's lisT

1. *Abbey Road* — The Beatles
2. *Innervisions* — Stevie Wonder
3. *Reckoning* — R.E.M.

DEan felBer's lIst

1. *Abbey Road* — The Beatles
2. *Murmur* — R.E.M.
3. *Physical Graffiti* — Led Zeppelin

jiM soNefeld's LiSt

1. *Moving Pictures* — Rush
2. *Blizzard of Ozz* — Ozzy Osbourne
3. *Vivid* — Living Colour

maRk BrYan's liSt

1. *Who's Next* — The Who
2. *Revolver* — The Beatles
3. *Let It Be* — The Replacements

My List

1 _____
2 _____
3 _____
4 _____
5 _____
6 _____
7 _____
8 _____
9 _____
10 _____

Best Rock album

103

bEsT rOck

1 "We Will Rock You" — Queen

2 "(I Can't Get No) Satisfaction" — The Rolling Stones

3 "Stairway to Heaven" — Led Zeppelin

4 "American Pie" — Don McLean

5 "Free Bird" — Lynyrd Skynyrd

6 "Rock and Roll All Night" — KISS

7 "Born to Be Wild" — Steppenwolf

8 "Another Brick in the Wall (Pt. II)" — Pink Floyd

9 "You Shook Me All Night Long" — AC/DC

10 "1999" — Prince
"Born to Run" — Bruce Springsteen

Just Missed
"I Love Rock 'n' Roll" — Joan Jett and the Blackhearts

"'You Shook Me All Night Long' is a rock anthem. Throughout history anthem's have just had a way of really reaching people and there's just so many songs along the way that just make you want to sing along and raise your fist in the air."

—Dee Snider, VH1 interview

anTHem

The Spy Who Shagged Me's
Verne Troyer (Mini Me)

veRne trOyer's LiSt

1. "Cowboy"   Kid Rock
2. "Nookie"   Limp Bizkit
3. "Man, I feel
   Like A Woman"   Shania Twain

> **''You Shook Me All Night Long' is the gentleman's club anthem of all time.''**
> **—Sugar Ray's Mark McGrath,**
> **VH1 interview**

anN wiLson's lisT

1. "Hey Jude"   The Beatles
2. "Stairway to Heaven"   Led Zeppelin
3. "Brown Sugar"   The Rolling Stones

naNcy wilSon's lIst

1. "Stairway to Heaven"   Led Zeppelin
2. "Hey Jude"   The Beatles
3. "Nights in White Satin"   The Moody Blues

My List

1 _____
2 _____
3 _____
4 _____
5 _____
6 _____
7 _____
8 _____
9 _____
10 _____

beSt RoCk anHEm

●─[bEsT rOck

#		
1	**Flea**	Red Hot Chili Peppers
2	**Paul McCartney**	The Beatles
3	**John Paul Jones**	Led Zeppelin
4	**Jason Newsted**	Metallica
5	**Sting**	The Police
6	**Gene Simmons**	KISS
7	**Roger Waters**	Pink Floyd
8	**John Entwistle**	The Who
9	**Bill Wyman**	The Rolling Stones
10	**Geddy Lee**	Rush

Just Missed
Les Claypool   Primus

FaCT

Aside from his regular gig with the Red Hot Chili Peppers, Flea has left his stamp on other artists' music, like Young MC's "Bust a Move" and Alanis Morissette's "You Oughta Know." Not content as a master of one instrument, he has also demonstrated his skills on the trumpet with Fishbone and on Jane's Addiction's "Idiots Rule."

bAss pLayEr

The Bass Player Gets the Girls.
soMe of geNe siMmons' woMen

1. Cher

2. Diana Ross

3. Liv Ullman

4. Shannon Tweed

My List

1. _____
2. _____
3. _____
4. _____
5. _____
6. _____
7. _____
8. _____
9. _____
10. _____

feMale arTist spEnd the

1. **Madonna**
2. **Shania Twain**
3. **Faith Hill**
4. **Gwen Stefani**
5. **Britney Spears**
6. **Stevie Nicks**
7. **Jennifer Lopez**
8. **Janet Jackson**
9. **Cher**
10. **Courtney Love**

Just Missed
Tina Turner

> **"I just compare it to all of the cheerleader, kiddie-porn types that are out there right now—Britney Spears and what not; I just think she blows the rest of them off the table."**
>
> —Anthrax's Scott Ian, on Gwen Stefani

yoU moSt waNt to niGht wiTh

waRren g'S LIst

1. Janet Jackson
2. Jennifer Lopez
3. Mariah Carey

chRistopher tiTus's liSt

1. Prince
2. Courtney Love
3. Patsy Cline

My List

1	
2	
3	
4	
5	
6	
7	
8	
9	
10	

BeSt '8os

> **"Madonna was dope, you know what I mean? To me, because her first record, I think that it was either 'Celebrate,' or 'Borderline.' Both of those two records were like hits in the 'hood. Those were black records to us."**
>
> —Queen Latifah, VH1 interview

1 **Madonna**

2 Duran Duran

3 Michael Jackson

4 Bon Jovi

5 U2

6 Guns N' Roses

7 The Police

8 Van Halen

9 Bruce Springsteen

10 Def Leppard

Just Missed
Prince

> **"They made it acceptable for me and my friends to go out and play air guitar in front of a boom box."**
>
> —actor Brad Rowe, on Van Halen

baNd or artiSt

artiSt wiTh moSt mulTiplatinum alBums

1. The Beatles	22
2. Elvis Presley	19
3. Garth Brooks; Led Zeppelin; Barbra Streisand; Van Halen	12
4. Aerosmith; Billy Joel; Elton John; Madonna, George Strait	11
5. Neil Diamond; Alabama; Pink Floyd; The Rolling Stones	10

Source: RIAA

pOison's brEt miChaels's liSt

1. Guns N' Roses
2. Metallica
3. Def Leppard

riCk JAmes's lisT

1. Michael Jackson
2. Madonna
3. Rick James

My List

1. _____
2. _____
3. _____
4. _____
5. _____
6. _____
7. _____
8. _____
9. _____
10. _____

> **"They're unmovable in their rhythm and blues touch."**
>
> —Ted Nugent. on Van Halen

best '80s Band or artist

111

mOst gro baNd or

1. **The Beatles**
2. **Elvis Presley**
3. **Jimi Hendrix**
4. **Nirvana**
5. **Led Zeppelin**
6. **Madonna**
7. **David Bowie**
8. **Bob Dylan**
9. **Black Sabbath**
10. **Pink Floyd**

Just Missed
Janis Joplin

> **"She's been right out there, right on the edge of where we only think about."**
>
> —Melissa Etheridge, on Madonna, VH1 interview

unDbreAking arTist

My List

1
2
3
4
5
6
7
8
9
10

bESt tV

1. *Cheers*
2. *Friends*
3. *The Monkees*
4. *Mission: Impossible*
5. *Happy Days*
6. *Scooby Doo*
7. *The Brady Bunch*
8. *Gilligan's Island*
9. *The Jeffersons*
10. *Welcome Back, Kotter*

Just Missed
The Simpsons

> **"It puts you in the mood to kill someone."**
>
> —actor John Stamos, on the *Friends* theme song

lIving cOlor's coRey gLoVer's liSt

1. *The Twilight Zone*
2. *Sanford and Son*
3. *The Jeffersons*

thEme soNg

1. *Peter Gunn*
2. *Perry Mason*
3. *One Day at a Time*

tEn arTists whO hAve appEared oN *thE siMpsons*

1. Aerosmith
2. Britney Spears
3. Cypress Hill
4. Paul McCartney
5. Red Hot Chili Peppers
6. Smashing Pumpkins
7. Spinal Tap
8. Sting
9. U2
10. The Who

My List

1.
2.
3.
4.
5.
6.
7.
8.
9.
10.

beSt tV thEme sOng

115

⊶[grEateSt

1. **John Lennon**

2. **Jimi Hendrix**

3. **Paul McCartney**

4. **Bob Dylan**

5. **Elvis Presley**

6. **Michael Jackson**

7. **Prince**

8. **Eric Clapton**

9. **David Bowie**

10. **Jim Morrison**

Just Missed
Kurt Cobain

❝He's got the American Dream going on, the good American boy. He brought rock and roll to the surface. He appropriated all of the sexy things from Motown and soul, and all of a sudden made it into the uptight white man's version: rock and roll.❞

—Smashing Pumpkins's Melissa Auf Der Maur, on Elvis Presley

geNius of rock aNd poP

athlete/model gaBrielle reeCe's liSt

1. Jimi Hendrix
2. Mick Jagger
3. Chuck Berry

"I would carry Bob Dylan's suitcase. I'd carry his guitar. To me, he's a great gift to this world."

—Bono, VH1 interview

My List

1.
2.
3.
4.
5.
6.
7.
8.
9.
10.

●─[grEatest

1 Elvis Presley

2 Jimi Hendrix

3 Jim Morrison

4 John Lennon

5 Paul McCartney

6 Bruce Springsteen

7 Steven Tyler

8 Eric Clapton

9 David Bowie

10 Mick Jagger

Just Missed
Sting; Kurt Cobain

> "Hands down, male or female, in the history of rock and roll, since I've been a child, it's Elvis Presley."
>
> —Smash Mouth's Steve Harwell, VH1 interview

mAle roCk stAr

liTtle riChard's LiSt

1. Michael Jackson
2. David Bowie
3. James Brown

shaRon lawrEnce's lIst

1. Mick Jagger
2. Sting
3. Bruce Springsteen

My List

1
2
3
4
5
6
7
8
9
10

●⊐[mOst eSs greAtest

1 **The Eagles** *Greatest Hits*

2 **The Beatles** *"Red Album/Blue Album"*

3 **Billy Joel** *Greatest Hits Volume I and Volume II*

4 **The Doors** *Greatest Hits*

5 **Madonna** *The Immaculate Collection*

6 **The Rolling Stones** *Hot Rocks*

7 **Fleetwood Mac** *Greatest Hits*

8 **Bob Marley** *Legend*

9 **Aerosmith** *Big Ones*

10 **U2** *The Best of...1980–1990*

Just Missed
KISS *Double Platinum*

❝It had a simple message that's timeless, that sort of spans generations. He's somebody I plan to listen to for the rest of my life.❞

—*Ally McBeal's* Gil Bellows, on Bob Marley

entiAL
hiTs collEction

frAnk deCaRo's liSt

1. Tina Turner   *Simply the Best*
2. Blondie   *The Platinum Collection*
3. Abba   *Gold*

> **"The real shame apart from Bob dying is that he was so big that the interest in reggae music went with him. He was reggae music as far as the world was concerned."**
>
> —Keith Richards, on Bob Marley, VH1 interview

My List

1.
2.
3.
4.
5.
6.
7.
8.
9.
10.

●─[mOst faS

1. **Madonna**

2. **David Bowie**

3. **Elton John**

4. **Will Smith**

5. **Cher**

6. **Gwen Stefani**

7. **Jennifer Lopez**

8. **Shania Twain**

9. **Ricky Martin**

10. **Prince**

Just Missed
Lenny Kravitz

> "I love Prince. He's an incredible musician. He sings beautifully. He's a great dancer. And, he's got style and he's very sexy."
>
> —Debbie Harry, VH1 interview

hioNable arTist

g. 10ve's liSt

1. Jimi Hendrix

2. Madonna

3. John Lee Hooker

> **"**I was into Motown and sophisticated urban soul. That's what was it for me. Even when I was ten, eleven years old, I wanted to be like the Temptations. I wanted to wear suits and the wrap-around cufflinks, and my mother used to [say], 'What do you want? What are you? An aspiring pimp?' I had the white shoes at eleven years old and the whole bit.**"**
>
> —Nile Rodgers, VH1 interview

My List

1
2
3
4
5
6
7
8
9
10

●─[grEatest

1 **Janis Joplin**

2 **Madonna**

3 **Tina Turner**

4 **Stevie Nicks**

5 **Cher**

6 **Debbie Harry**

7 **Chrissie Hynde**

8 **Alanis Morissette**

9 **Grace Slick**

10 **Gwen Stefani**

Just Missed
Courtney Love

Moby, Andy Dick, and Gavin Rossdale get rowdy on the set.

feMale roCk stAr

buSh's gavIn rosSdale's liSt
....
1. Janis Joplin

2. Siouxie Sioux

3. Patti Smith

moBy's LIst
....
1. P.J. Harvey

2. Courtney Love

3. Kim Gordon

My List

1 _____

2 _____

3 _____

4 _____

5 _____

6 _____

7 _____

8 _____

9 _____

10 _____

mOst inF baNd or

1. **The Beatles**
2. **Elvis Presley**
3. **Jimi Hendrix**
4. **Led Zeppelin**
5. **Madonna**
6. **Bob Dylan**
7. **Nirvana**
8. **Eric Clapton**
9. **David Bowie**
10. **Chuck Berry**

Just Missed
Queen

luenTial arTist

> 66He was really a genius and it ushered in a slew of really depressing sad songs that you love to listen to over and over again.99
>
> —actress Tia Carrere, on Kurt Cobain

brAd rOwe's liSt

1. Led Zeppelin
2. Van Halen
3. Jimi Hendrix

> 66None of the black artists had dancers in those days, and it was like Madonna came out with these dancers and the next thing you know everybody had dancers.99
>
> —Nile Rodgers, VH1 interview

My List

1. _____
2. _____
3. _____
4. _____
5. _____
6. _____
7. _____
8. _____
9. _____
10. _____

●─[seXieSt

1. Madonna
2. Shania Twain
3. Faith Hill
4. Tina Turner
5. Gwen Stefani
6. Jennifer Lopez
7. Britney Spears
8. Janet Jackson
9. Stevie Nicks
10. Toni Braxton

Just Missed
Vanessa Williams

> **"If this place was on fire and they told you to haul ass, she would have to make ten trips."**
>
> —hip-hop artist Warren G., on Jennifer Lopez

feMale aRtist

Gloria Reuben and Meat Loaf

meAt loAf's LiSt

1. Marilyn Monroe
2. Janis Joplin
3. Olivia Newton-John

"Very sexy, very smart, very creative, gorgeous, she knows how to work it."

—Rick James, on Madonna

My List

1.
2.
3.
4.
5.
6.
7.
8.
9.
10.

sexiest feMale artist

⊶[seXieSt

1. **Elvis Presley**
2. **Ricky Martin**
3. **Jon Bon Jovi**
4. **Jim Morrison**
5. **Sting**
6. **Enrique Iglesias**
7. **Lenny Kravitz**
8. **Prince**
9. **Gavin Rossdale**
10. **Rob Thomas**

Just Missed
Will Smith

FaCT

Sting, who once boasted he could sustain lovemaking for a number of hours at a time using the Tantric method, now says he's given up Tantric sex. "What I'm trying to get Trudi into now is Tantric shopping, where you go shopping for five hours and you don't buy anything."

mAle aRtist

meLissa aUf deR maUr's liSt

1. Morrissey
2. Prince
3. Elvis Presley

"I had never gotten it; like, I knew everyone said he was sex on a stick. Whatever. But seeing him live, every man and woman in that room was physically turned on by that performance. He was having sex in front of you. And it's like a deviant kind of sexual and he's kinda got a gospel God-thing going on."

—Melissa Auf Der Maur, on Prince

My List

1
2
3
4
5
6
7
8
9
10

⊶[seXieSt

1	**"Wicked Game"**	Chris Isaak
2	**"Justify My Love"**	Madonna
3	**"Hungry Like the Wolf"**	Duran Duran
4	**"Breathe"**	Faith Hill
5	**"Crazy"**	Aerosmith
6	**"Living La Vida Loca"**	Ricky Martin
7	**"Cradle of Love"**	Billy Idol
8	**"Girls Girls Girls"**	Motley Crue
9	**"Addicted to Love"**	Robert Palmer
10	**"Sexual Healing"**	Marvin Gaye

Just Missed
"Kiss"   Prince

❝She's so hot in this video it's frightening.❞

—Goo Goo Dolls's Johnny Rzeznik, on
   Madonna's "Justify My Love" video

muSic vidEo

❝You feel like you're doing something wrong just watching it.❞

—singer Montell Jordan, on Madonna's "Justify My Love" video

moNtell joRdan's lisT

1. "Hold On"   En Vogue
2. "Justify My Love"   Madonna
3. "Baby Got Back"   Sir Mix-a-Lot

❝I had to go take a shower after I watched this.❞

—actress Kari Wuhrer on Madonna's "Justify My Love" video

My List

1
2
3
4
5
6
7
8
9
10

seXiEst MusiC viDEo

133

○─[best '70s

1 "Stairway to Heaven" — Led Zeppelin

2 "Hotel California" — The Eagles

3 "Imagine" — John Lennon

4 "Bohemian Rhapsody" — Queen

5 "American Pie" — Don McLean

6 "Free Bird" — Lynyrd Skynyrd

7 "Born to Run" — Bruce Springsteen

8 "Layla" — Derek and the Dominoes

9 "Stayin' Alive" — Bee Gees

10 "I Will Survive" — Gloria Gaynor

Just Missed
"What's Going On" — Marvin Gaye

"Every girl I wanted to sleep with made me listen to this song."
—David Alan Grier, on "American Pie"

David Alan Grier

soNg

toP hiTs of tHe 197os		(weeks at #1)
1. "You Light Up My Life"	Debby Boone	10
2. "Night Fever"	Bee Gees	8
"Tonight's the Night (Gonna Be Alright)"	Rod Stewart	8
3. "Shadow Dancing"	Andy Gibb	7
4. "Freak"	Chic	6
"My Sharona"	The Knack	6
"The First Time Ever I Saw Your Face"	Roberta Flack	6
"Alone Again (Naturally)"	Gilbert O'Sullivan	6
"Joy to the World"	Three Dog Night	6
"Bridge Over Troubled Water"	Simon and Garfunkel	6

Source: *Billboard*

actrEss daNa delAny's liSt

1. "What's Going On"   Marvin Gaye
2. "Alison"   Elvis Costello
3. "Mr. Big Stuff"   Jean Knight

My List

1. _____
2. _____
3. _____
4. _____
5. _____
6. _____
7. _____
8. _____
9. _____
10. _____

Best '70s soNg

gReateSt

1. **Aretha Franklin**

2. **Tina Turner**

3. **Cher**

4. **Barbra Streisand**

5. **Diana Ross**

6. **Bette Midler**

7. **Stevie Nicks**

8. **Whitney Houston**

9. **Celine Dion**

10. **Shania Twain**

Just Missed
Mariah Carey

> **"**An artist like Diana represented really as high up on the food chain as you get. As high up on the artist chain. She continues to be an important figure in my life.**"**
>
> —Nile Rodgers, on Diana Ross

diVa

liSa lOeb's lIst

1. Barbra Streisand
2. Elton John
3. Cher

trAci loRds's liSt

1. Tina Turner
2. Deborah Harry
3. Shirley Manson

eD mcMAhon's lISt

1. Billie Holiday
2. Aretha Franklin
3. Eartha Kitt

"If you can just say a single name, you know you're there. Now, this woman commands a stage. When she gets on a stage, a lot of singers come up and sing a song, this woman sings the whole stage and she's like a walking boa. And it's one name: Aretha."

—Ed McMahon

My List

1. _____
2. _____
3. _____
4. _____
5. _____
6. _____
7. _____
8. _____
9. _____
10. _____

greAtest diVa

beSt roCk

1	**John Bonham**	Led Zeppelin
2	**Lars Ulrich**	Metallica
3	**Keith Moon**	The Who
4	**Tommy Lee**	Motley Crüe
5	**Phil Collins**	
6	**Ringo Starr**	The Beatles
7	**Alex Van Halen**	Van Halen
8	**Dave Grohl**	Nirvana
	Mick Fleetwood	Fleetwood Mac
9	**Neil Peart**	Rush
10	**Chad Smith**	Red Hot Chili Peppers

Just Missed
Charlie Watts   The Rolling Stones

faCT

John Bonham never took drum lessons.

druMmer

FacT
Keith Moon was the inspiration for the Muppets's drummer Animal.

drUmmers wHo tooK thE leAd

1. Phil Collins

2. Don Henley

3. Karen Carpenter

4. Dave Grohl

My List

1.
2.
3.
4.
5.
6.
7.
8.
9.
10.

Best rocK drummer

139

⊶[bEst siNg

1. **John Lennon**
2. **Paul McCartney**
3. **Bob Dylan**
4. **Prince**
5. **Bruce Springsteen**
6. **Stevie Nicks**
7. **Carole King**
8. **Stevie Wonder**
9. **James Taylor**
10. **Sarah McLachlan**

Just Missed
Neil Young

> **"He's an incredible song writer, he's a totally imitated singer, and his stuff is still so current today that they're still using it in all the rap stuff, and I think he was the leader of that sound."**
>
> —Rick Springfield, on Stevie Wonder

> **"He speaks to the common man in those terms and people relate to those characters and there's a sense of redemption in his songs. He's just a divine inspiration for me."**
>
> —Sheryl Crow, on Bob Dylan, VH1 interview

giL bEllows's liSt

1. John Lennon
2. Bob Dylan
3. Bob Marley

jaSon falKner's lISt

1. David Bowie
2. Ray Davies
3. Paul Simon

> **"George Strait is why I play country music. Why I play music other than God and my family is James Taylor."**
>
> —Garth Brooks, VH1 interview

My List

1	
2	
3	
4	
5	
6	
7	
8	
9	
10	

bEst soNg

1 "Imagine" — John Lennon

2 "Bohemian Rhapsody" — Queen

3 "Hotel California" — The Eagles

4 "Hey Jude" — The Beatles

5 "American Pie" — Don McLean
"(I Can't Get No) Satisfaction" — The Rolling Stones

6 "Stairway to Heaven" — Led Zeppelin

7 "Smells Like Teen Spirit" — Nirvana

8 "Respect" — Aretha Franklin

9 "(Sittin' On) The Dock of the Bay" — Otis Redding

10 "Born to Run" — Bruce Springsteen

Just Missed
"I Got You (I Feel Good)" — James Brown

"The last song of the night: When you would slink up to whoever it was you were slinking up into, you'd kinda grab her and go in a circle. That's got to be number one."

—Skid Row's Sebastian Bach, on "Stairway to Heaven"

meLissa ethEridge's liSt

1. "Born to Run"   Bruce Springsteen
2. "In Your Eyes"   Peter Gabriel
3. "You Oughta Know"   Alanis Morissette

❝It was like hearing Shakespeare in rock and roll. It was intense, and romantic, and rebellious. I was fourteen, it was perfect. It saved my life. That song, I think, is just the perfect rock and roll song.❞

—Melissa Etheridge, on "Born to Run"

FaCT

Two months after he died in a plane crash, "(Sittin' On) The Dock of the Bay" became Otis Redding's first and only number one single.

frEnch steWart's LIst

1. "Respect"   Aretha Franklin
2. "Hey Joe"   Jimi Hendrix Experience
3. "That's What I Like
   About You"   The Romantics

My List

1 _____
2 _____
3 _____
4 _____
5 _____
6 _____
7 _____
8 _____
9 _____
10 _____

Best Song

⊶[beSt soN

1. **John Lennon and Paul McCartney**
2. **Bernie Taupin and Elton John**
3. **Bob Dylan**
4. **Barry, Robin, and Maurice Gibb**
5. **Prince; Carole King** (tied)
6. **Mick Jagger and Keith Richards**
7. **Brian Wilson**
8. **Bruce Springsteen**
9. **Paul Simon**
10. **Stevie Wonder**

Just Missed
Van Morrison; James Taylor; Bob Marley

❝That song really takes you on a journey. It's sort of like you have a special lens that you put on when you hear that song, and everything looks different, and you're going through this day where obviously you're slightly altered in some way, and it's very objective in an interesting way. And of course the balance between the John Lennon lyrics and then Paul McCartney's middle part is so great.❞

—Nancy Wilson, on "Strawberry Fields Forever," VH1 interview

gwRiter

jaNis iaN's lIst

1. Leonard Cohen
2. Radiohead
3. Marianne Faithfull

My List

1. _____
2. _____
3. _____
4. _____
5. _____
6. _____
7. _____
8. _____
9. _____
10. _____

Best songwriter

grEatest

1 "Summer Nights" John Travolta and Olivia Newton-John

2 "I Got You Babe" Sonny and Cher

3 "Unforgettable" Natalie Cole and Nat "King" Cole

4 "Walk This Way" Run-D.M.C. with Steven Tyler and Joe Perry

5 "Under Pressure" Queen and David Bowie

6 "Stop Draggin' My Heart Around" Stevie Nicks and Tom Petty

7 "(I've Had) The Time of My Life" Bill Medley and Jennifer Warnes

8 "Endless Love" Lionel Ritchie and Diana Ross

9 "Up Where We Belong" Joe Cocker and Jennifer Warnes

10 "Don't Let the Sun Go Down on Me" Elton John and George Michael

Just Missed
"You Don't Bring Me Flowers" Neil Diamond and Barbra Streisand

dUet

joEy McIntyRe's liSt
....
1. "Unforgettable" Natalie Cole and Nat "King" Cole
2. "Where Is the Love"   Roberta Flack and
                              Donny Hathaway
3. "You Don't Bring Me Flowers" Neil Diamond
                        and Barbra Streisand

elLen cleGhorn's LIst
....
1. "Don't Let the Sun Go Down On Me"
                  Elton John and George Michael
2. "Whatta Man"   Salt-n-Pepa and En Vogue
3. "Music of My Heart"   'NSYNC and
                              Gloria Estefan

My List
1 _____
2 _____
3 _____
4 _____
5 _____
6 _____
7 _____
8 _____
9 _____
10 _____

greATest

1	**Paul McCartney**
2	**Bob Dylan**
3	**Aretha Franklin**
4	**Eric Clapton**
5	**Elton John**
6	**B. B. King**
7	**Madonna**
8	**Tina Turner**
9	**Michael Jackson**
10	**David Bowie**

Just Missed
Jimmy Page

FacT
Of all the artists listed above, only Michael Jackson and Madonna are not yet fifty years old.

"He just changed my life. I still think he's one of the most important artists of the millennium, of any millennium."

—Bonnie Raitt, on Bob Dylan,
VH1 interview

LiVing legEnd

loRi peTty's LiSt

1. Madonna
2. Michael Jackson
3. Aretha Franklin

scOtt HAmilton's liSt

1. Quincy Jones
2. Paul McCartney
3. Bruce Springsteen

My List

1 _____
2 _____
3 _____
4 _____
5 _____
6 _____
7 _____
8 _____
9 _____
10 _____

Greatest Living Legend

mAle arTist spEnd the

1. Jon Bon Jovi
2. Ricky Martin
3. Sting
4. David Bowie; Anthony Kiedis
5. Steven Tyler
6. Mark McGrath
7. Will Smith
8. Bono
9. Lenny Kravitz
10. Chris Isaak

Just Missed
Gavin Rossdale

yoU moSt waNt to niGht wiTh

> **"I would eat broken glass for him. He also seems like a big pervert and that's a plus."**
>
> —The Go-Go's Jane Wiedlin, on David Bowie

Bush's Gavin Rossdale

My List

1 _____
2 _____
3 _____
4 _____
5 _____
6 _____
7 _____
8 _____
9 _____
10 _____

❝Well, it wiped out world hunger, that's for sure.❞

—Spinal Tap's Derek Smalls, on Live Aid

Spinal Tap

ificAnt moMent rOll

> **"**You can barely understand the words; the guy sings at all different times; he doesn't know when to come in; and this song sold twelve million copies. Why? Because this song said 'rock and roll.' It's not about perfection, it's about attitude.**"**
>
> —Martha Quinn, on "Louie Louie"

spInal tAp's DAvid sT. huBbins's liSt

1. David and Nigel Tufnel

2. KISS with and without makeup

3. Phil Spector/echoButton

> **"**It immediately made the coal-burning guitar obsolete.**"**
>
> —"Weird Al" Yankovic, on Les Paul's invention of the electric guitar

cOolio's LIst

1. Run-D.M.C. Covering "Walk This Way"

2. Lollapalooza Adding Hip-Hop to the Lineup

3. The Death of Jerry Garcia

> **"**It's a double-edged sword because it made people watch music as opposed to listen to it. So the interpretation of music changed.**"**
>
> —Dweezil Zappa, on MTV, VH1 interview

My List

1 _____
2 _____
3 _____
4 _____
5 _____
6 _____
7 _____
8 _____
9 _____
10 _____

my liSts

My List

1 _____
2 _____
3 _____
4 _____
5 _____
6 _____
7 _____
8 _____
9 _____
10 _____

My List

1 _____
2 _____
3 _____
4 _____
5 _____
6 _____
7 _____
8 _____
9 _____
10 _____

My List

1 _____
2 _____
3 _____
4 _____
5 _____
6 _____
7 _____
8 _____
9 _____
10 _____

My List

1 _____
2 _____
3 _____
4 _____
5 _____
6 _____
7 _____
8 _____
9 _____
10 _____

My List

1 _____
2 _____
3 _____
4 _____
5 _____
6 _____
7 _____
8 _____
9 _____
10 _____

My List

1 _____
2 _____
3 _____
4 _____
5 _____
6 _____
7 _____
8 _____
9 _____
10 _____

my liSts

My List
1. _____
2. _____
3. _____
4. _____
5. _____
6. _____
7. _____
8. _____
9. _____
10. _____

My List
1. _____
2. _____
3. _____
4. _____
5. _____
6. _____
7. _____
8. _____
9. _____
10. _____

My List
1. _____
2. _____
3. _____
4. _____
5. _____
6. _____
7. _____
8. _____
9. _____
10. _____

My List

1. _____
2. _____
3. _____
4. _____
5. _____
6. _____
7. _____
8. _____
9. _____
10. _____

My List

1. _____
2. _____
3. _____
4. _____
5. _____
6. _____
7. _____
8. _____
9. _____
10. _____

My List

1. _____
2. _____
3. _____
4. _____
5. _____
6. _____
7. _____
8. _____
9. _____
10. _____

 my liSts

My List

1
2
3
4
5
6
7
8
9
10

My List

1
2
3
4
5
6
7
8
9
10

My List

1
2
3
4
5
6
7
8
9
10

My List

1 _____
2 _____
3 _____
4 _____
5 _____
6 _____
7 _____
8 _____
9 _____
10 _____

My List

1 _____
2 _____
3 _____
4 _____
5 _____
6 _____
7 _____
8 _____
9 _____
10 _____

My List

1 _____
2 _____
3 _____
4 _____
5 _____
6 _____
7 _____
8 _____
9 _____
10 _____

Presenting the companion books to one of television's most popular series!

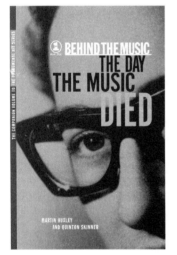
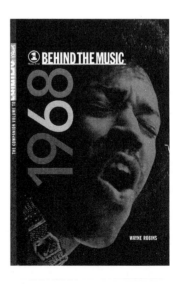